THE RESULTS MAP

The Results Map
Business and Life strategies to get what you want
Copyright© 2014 Kimberly Alexander
www.KimberlyAlexanderInc.com

Library of Congress Control Number: 2014904719

ISBN: 978-0-9960007-0-3

1. Business / Sustainable Development
2. Business / Strategic Planning
3. Business / Time Management

QUANTITY PURCHASES: Companies, professional groups, clubs, and other organizations may qualify for special terms when ordering quantities of this title. For information e-mail Kimberly@KimberlyAlexanderInc.com

This book is printed in the United States of America.

THE RESULTS MAP

Business and Life strategies to get what you want

Kimberly Alexander

DEDICATION

For my husband JJ
With you, everything is possible

CONTENTS

INTRODUCTION

MAY 8, 2012 WAS A LIFE-CHANGING DAY FOR ME; I decided to write this book. I was discussing with my husband, some great motivational speakers and how they have made an impact on people's lives. I told him, "I think I have a lot to share about what I do best." My husband looked me dead in the eye and simply said, "Write a book." I started a file on my computer titled Future book. Defining moments, learning lessons, experiences I had, anything that came to mind I kept an on-going list of what I could write about and share. I thought a book would come to light someday, and knew I would make it happen when the timing was right.

Then, it happened again, on September 22, 2013, I was sharing with my sister Elizabeth some thoughts I had about possibilities for my future, my passions and what I loved to do. She too responded, "Write a book." Throughout that summer, I offered to help some companies with challenges they were facing and individual business owners in times of opportunity and challenge because I simply care about people and to see companies succeed. Toward the end of that season, many influential community leaders that I respect, came to me and told me that I should make a business out of what I was coaching to. More people kept sharing the same idea. That was it, so many neon signs now flashing in front of me, to share what I love to do, and that is to help people and companies build to their fullest potential.

With my family, my mentors and my friends by my side, full belief in my heart and head, I jumped into the sea of opportunity and have never looked back. My destiny is to live my best life, as I teach others to do the same. To help companies seek new opportunities and grow because of them. My plan is to bring flashing neon signs to you too.

Time to start your journey…

Executive Summary

THE RESULTS MAP IS A SET OF STEPS AND FUNDA-mentals that will guide you on your journey to success and the life you want to live. As with any map it can be used as a tool to get you from point A to point B. Exercises and action steps will guide you on how to reach your goals. You will be taking action in these areas to move through your map, beginning at the starting point, working through your journey with the end result discovering your hidden treasure, that being your results.

You may discover challenges along the way, taking a wrong turn, skipping over steps and even taking a stumble or fall here and there. Get back up, brush yourself off, and re-plot your course. Follow the proven process that has helped hundreds of leaders navigate to the results they have been hunting for. You can do it too.

Chapter 1: The Starting Point

In Chapter one you will gain a clear understanding of the three fundamentals of The Road Map: perspective, strategy and results and why they are important in your journey.

Chapter 2: Change Course

Before you begin, you will need to do some searching to find all the right tools for your trek. You will need to be aware of the importance of making sound choices. Making a choice is one thing, making the right one (or avoiding them) can dramatically affect your business in either a positive or negative way. In chapter two, learn steps to take action.

Often, tough choices come when we set out to make changes. Allow yourself to open up to new ideas and strategies. Although challenging, the need to change may be the reason why you picked up this book or identified the need for a different plan. Whatever reason, you are sure to experience different results from making even the smallest of changes. Change has the possibility of bringing great rewards.

Chapter 3: Your Crew

It is almost impossible to embark on any journey without a crew: your team of people that will help you get to where you plan to go. In chapter three, learn how to find the right team and get them on board to put your plans in motion through the four I's: Identify, Inspire, Influence and Impact. If you envision trudging through the map on your own, you will not find your treasure. It takes a team to reach your destination.

Chapter 4: Beyond the Horizon

In Chapter four you will establish the purpose of your journey. You cannot head up the hill or set sail unless you understand where you are heading and why you want to get there. In chapter four, you will identify and understand what you want to accomplish both professionally and personally. When identifying your planned accomplishments you will ask yourself three questions: Will it make a positive impact on my business and life? Will it make me proud? Without it, will I be fulfilled? Identifying "what" you want and "why" will drive you. The "when" and "who" will help you plan your route. This chapter contains simple yet intensive exercises that must be completed before you move ahead.

Chapter 5: Vision and Strategy

As you embark on your journey, you will read in chapter five how to identify how you plan and take action. Doing so will bring awareness to your actions and how you can maximize your potential. There will be stumbling blocks along the way, or a fork in the road. Do you trudge ahead without thinking or stop and assess every situation? Both traits influence how you plan and take action and are equally important. Recognizing when to rely on each of those strengths could make the difference in reaching the summit or staying in base camp. Understanding who you are is an important element to take you over the next hurdle and to keep going.

Chapter 6: Chart Your Course

In chapter six you will learn how to chart your course and plan your strategy. This can be an uphill climb, but the view from the top will be worth it. In this chapter you will learn to identify non-negotiable and negotiable activities and how to make a sound plan with them to achieve your planned accomplishments. You have two options when building your strategy:

Option 1: You can keep the hours and time frame to work toward your planned accomplishments based on the needs of your business and life.

Option 2: You can adjust the hours and time frame by moving your planned accomplishments based on the needs of your business and life.

You will work through exercises to chart the smartest course that will work for you.

Chapter 7: Boundaries

In chapter seven you will learn steps for setting boundaries on your time: a critical element to your Results Map. You may have the best plan and people in place, but if you don't have the right amount of time assigned to it, will you realistically be able to achieve what you set out to do? In this chapter you will work through exercises to learn how to mirror your time with your planned accomplishments.

Chapter 8: Systems in Place

In chapter eight, we find another mountain to climb, but you are getting closer to the summit. You will learn how to establish systems within different timeframes to effectively manage your Results Map using daily, weekly and monthly calendars.

Chapter 9: Launch

In Chapter nine you will cross the bridge from reaction to action. You are ready to put your Results Map to work. This can take great discipline and continued follow through. In this chapter you will crosscheck all that you have learned to ensure that every system is in sync, always with the principle of mirroring your time to your planned accomplishments.

Chapter 10: The Journey Continues

Congratulations! You have reached the treasure. The question is, do you keep the treasure for good, or will it dwindle on your trek home? Changing behaviors can be dramatic and although your plan and action steps are in place, you can still take a fall or slip into old habits. Stay the course and spot check your progress and results. You may need to make tweaks along the way. Chapter ten will guide you through making changes for the better and for long term growth.

Let's get started.

Chapter 1

The Starting Point

"Step Back. Imagine the Possibilities. Create the Plan.
Enjoy the Process. Relish the Outcome."
— Successories

PEOPLE ARE LOOKING FOR QUICK AND EASY AN-swers: The brass key. The golden ticket. The right formula. You've spent weeks if not years of time working to get that big break and it never comes...Why? You may have everything in place from people, to marketing, to products and services, to systems, to vendors and still you can't seem to hit the numbers. You increase staff, decrease staff, cut costs, spend more, and add promotion after promotion. The plan still isn't matching your ambitions. You question what is going wrong, when, more importantly, you should take inventory of what is going right.

The Results Map is a series of exercises that will enable you to chart a course to the business you want to build and the life you want to live. You will not find all of your answers on one page. Trust the process. What you will learn are the fundamentals needed to make decisions and change behaviors in order to bring you the outcome you are looking for. In this chapter you will learn the main fundamentals of The Results Map and why they are important to building your plan. Throughout the book, this fundamental learning and the exercises to follow will form your Map.

Let me give you a couple of scenarios. First scenario: you've been looking for your sunglasses around the house for ten minutes and, low and behold, they rest comfortably on your head.

Second scenario: You're late for a meeting and after digging through your entire office, you find that your documents were in your bag the entire time. Sound familiar?

Although these examples are simplistic, the same is true when looking for answers to your business goals. They are right in front of you, but you just can't see them yet. Before you spend another dime or dream up another promotion, stop and read.

THE ANSWERS LIE WITHIN THE PERSPECTIVES, STRATEGIES AND ACTIONS OF YOU AND THE PEOPLE WITHIN YOUR COMPANY.

Brilliance is waiting and it's closer than you can ever imagine. What does the company, division or team that you want, need or dream of look like? If you could have the business of your dreams, would you make changes to get it? Do you even know where to start? Could the results you are seeing now be elevated, enhanced, and made bigger? The difference of seeing results versus dreaming of them is perspective and the willingness to change.

Before you set out a quest to find results, I'm going to share with you my story of how this book came to life. Reinventing my professional goals was a journey, and what I needed was a map to get me there. It involved changing my perspective on the nature and purpose behind my work, and resulting shifts in my personal and professional strategies. I decided to share the tools I developed and used to see increased results, so that anyone could do the same.

Since birth, I have been an overachiever. I am an out of the box, can-do-*more* person. I strive and drive to be the best in all that I do. Now, there have been times that this has gotten me ahead and there have been times that it was downright unhealthy. Just because you are a driver doesn't mean you always win and, often times, doesn't get you more.

I worked for a company that I believed in and I put in the hours because of that belief. But more than that, I had a need to make a difference. So, I ran through airports, gave 150% of myself 15 to 18 hours a day and put every last ounce of energy into "the job." Sadly, what I put very little into was my own personal development and life. Every ounce of energy went into building and achieving results. My incredible husband and children, my health, my family and friends, and even my home took a back seat. My team started noticing a change in me, that I am sure led them to disappointment and concern. The over-achiever in me was transforming into an under-achiever. The life that I dreamed of was vanishing. In a nutshell, I lost all perspective on my work. I had severe tunnel vision and couldn't see what was in front of me. The problem wasn't simply that I wasn't seeing the results I wanted, but also that my relationships were floundering and I was losing myself in the job. Everything in my life was being driven by the numbers, the bottom line, and growth forecasts. I was literally losing my sense of who I was.

One weekend I was home and very, very tired. I had fallen asleep while reading a book to my little girls, and my husband, with tears in his eyes, told me that he missed me. I got on the scale and I was 30 pounds heavier. I felt lousy mentally and physically. So, I asked myself, "How did I get here?" I sat and reflected on previous months with my team and peers and how hard I had started to drive them, all to get the numbers. I was losing sleep, crying daily, working harder, going backward and living in a reaction mode. At that moment, I decided to change my perspective. Otherwise, I would simply lose everything. So that is what I did...

I CHOSE TO CHANGE MY PERSPECTIVE.

My expectations of what the perfect job looked like and what it took to get results were very different. I wanted less travel and task-oriented duties; I needed to put people first and find balance. Yes, balance. That was my deal maker, not the money or the title, but to be present in everything I did. No more running, no more reaction mode. Perspective and strategy were what I needed.

I asked myself what was driving me to over-achieve? Why did I have this need to excel without regard to my needs or those of my loved ones? I needed to find a way to compromise and get the sense of professional satisfaction I wanted without damaging my health and my relationships. After all, being a driver isn't bad; it's keeping that drive in check that matters.

So, I cut unnecessary tasks and was streamlining my focus on my team's strengths and what needed to be accomplished. Work smarter not harder was an understatement. Simplistic approaches, high level support and training, strong follow through and more balance. We made the numbers and I had a life too, go figure! Almost immediately, I started seeing changes for the better. I was also more present in my life. With less chaos and craziness at work I was able to focus on the most important areas of my life: my family, my friends, my health and my sense of self. It takes discipline to change and get the results you want, but with a clear, strategic plan and perspective, you will get there.

FROM MY OWN EXPERIENCES AND LEARNING I DEVELOPED THE RESULTS MAP PROCESS.

I suppose that my story isn't anything you haven't read before. And that's the point. This story repeats itself again and again in the business community, and it's time for professionals to make a change. That change starts with you.

The Results Map begins with three simple yet powerful fundamentals:

PERSPECTIVE, STRATEGY AND RESULTS.

This book will guide you through these three areas in order to plan your Results Map. From one map to the next, every person's plan will have similarities, but will be very different. Everyone is sailing toward different goals, with varied skill sets, perspectives, demands and even dreams. One thing to be mindful of is to follow the process. Don't skip over chapters. Allow yourself the growth needed to work toward the Results Map you desire.

THE ANSWERS LIE WITHIN THIS BOOK, TRUST ME.

> ➢ Perspective will bring you self –discovery and help establish boundaries and protected time.
> ➢ Strategy will put your plan and systems into place.
> ➢ Results will be driven by your actions.

We will go deeper throughout the book, exploring each fundamental noted above and laying the foundation of your Results Map. As you are reading, keep a few things in mind:

> ➢ This book is not a quick fix, but a guide that will require continuous tweaks and follow up.
> ➢ You will be learning strategies alongside tools to get you to where you want to be.
> ➢ You are working to end less productive habits and create new, effective habits. Be patient. It takes time to change.
> ➢ Change can be challenging. However, it can bring great rewards.
> ➢ Learn from your past to thrive in your present and future.

Throughout the book there will be learning, exercises and action items. You have chosen to start down the road. Taking the steps to develop your Results Map will help you understand and achieve the outcomes in life and business that you desire. I want to see that happen for you.

SEE IT THROUGH AND DON'T GIVE UP.

Write, highlight, scribble, cross out and write again. Do the work and the rewards will come.

You have one life to live, so make it your best. Now let's get to work.

Main Message

➢ The foundation of The Results Map starts with three simple yet powerful fundamentals: perspective, strategy and results. They will guide you as you approach each exercise and build your Road Map to success.

➢ Follow the proven process. Read every chapter and do not skip activities.

Notes

CHAPTER 2
CHANGE COURSE
———————

*"Life is about Choices. Large or small, our actions forge our futures,
hopefully inspiring others along the way."*
– Howard Schultz, CEO, Starbucks

THE RESULTS MAP FUNDAMENTAL: PERSPECTIVE

Life comes with making choices and changes. One choice can change the entire outcome of your business and life. Being clear on why and how you make choices is important in developing your Results Map. In this chapter we will discuss the power of making tough choices the right way in order to change and grow your business and life.

People often forget that they have the power not only to make choices, but to own them and take action on them. The average person makes up to 35,000 choices per day. That probably seems like a lot of choices, but think about the process of going out for dinner. First, you decide where to go and what time, then table or booth, what to drink, get an appetizer, decide on dinner choice, soup or salad, finish your plate or get a to go box. That's eight decisions, just for dinner. And in reality, you probably make more choices than that when you go out to eat! We make choices by the minute, all day, every day.

So what happens when you come to a choice that isn't as easy as picking a soup or a salad? Let me give you another example. Have you ever been stuck considering if you should pitch a deal to a prospective client? Are you qualified? Do you have the staff in place to manage the deal if you got it? How should you cost it out? Will your decisions inhibit growth within other accounts? The list goes on. Making choices and changes can be challenging when you are not clear where you are heading or where it is that you want to land.

Making choices is easier when you are clear in what you want and understand the steps you need to take to get there.

An average of twenty-seven choices per day take up to nine minutes to make. That's four hours of contemplation time each day. That is a lot of brain-power clouding up clarity and leaving you frustrated about your next steps. Have you ever come home to your family at the end of the day only to be asked, "what do you want for dinner?" You then dive into a deep spiral and proclaim you cannot make one more single decision! This should be a clear sign that you are struggling to make choices. But you're not alone. Everybody gets tired of making choices. They can be exhausting to make.

This does not mean that clarifying your Results Map will spare you difficult choices. Instead, you will just be more confident in making them.

For example, I was offered a long term, high level consulting contract with a company. It would be more money than I had made in my career prior, and a great opportunity to exercise everything I had done in my past. I turned it down in about two minutes flat. Was I crazy? No, I wasn't. The quick and easy route would have been to take the immediate offering: the easy road. After hearing the offer, I was able to turn it down because it was not a part of my Results Map and planned accomplishments. Financially it was the immediate win, but would take me off track and away from what I wanted to accomplish long term. I wanted to reach broad audiences, help multiple companies and executives grow and prosper, and speak to hundreds of people about the message of this book. I could not accomplish that if I dedicated all of my time to one company. This is a prime example of being crystal clear in knowing what you want in order to make the right choices. Don't get me wrong, immediate wins can bring short term and long term gain, but these gains should always be considered alongside your Results Map.

THE QUESTION YOU NEED TO ASK YOURSELF IS, "DOES IT FALL IN LINE WITH MY PLANNED ACCOMPLISHMENTS?"

There are several areas that can make decision making difficult. First, let's touch on guilt and victimization.

Let's start with guilt. Have you ever been focused on eating healthy, and on day two, you break down and eat a cupcake at a party or have a martini with dinner? You chose to deviate from your plan. With every drink or bite you feel like you've failed; not even enjoying the treat in front of you. This can be incredibly damaging. When you are making strong, clear choices, it can alleviate these negative emotions and behaviors.

WHEN YOU MAKE A CHOICE, LIVE IN IT, RELISH IN IT, OWN IT!

If you are going to veer from your plan, own the decision. Enjoy the drink or the cupcake and reset your mind. Don't focus on the failure, instead focus on how to get back on course the next day. We beat ourselves up too often. Whenever you tell yourself, "I can't," "I failed," I will never," etc., your brain will remember and believe it. Be kind to yourself and instead of all of that negative talk, say, "I can and I will."

YOU WILL NOT BELIEVE HOW EMPOWERED YOU WILL FEEL BY OWNING YOUR CHOICES.

One thing to caution you on: just because you are crystal clear on making and owning your choices, doesn't mean that you can make them without consideration of how they affect other people. Your journey will affect many, so always make your choices wisely and responsibly.

Next is the victim card. Do you understand that you have the right to make choices and have the ability to make changes? I don't intend to sound condescending, but want to bring the awareness that yes, you do! The sense of "victimization" sits deep inside and can poison our sense of our own accomplishments and disempower us from making the correct choices in life and in the workplace.

Some people wallow in the sense of victimization and it is almost impossible to move forward when it happens. For example, you were running late and missed an appointment because there was traffic and you lost a deal. You curse the traffic, but really, you didn't allow for traffic time. Being a victim is really about a lack of accountability. Everything is everyone else's fault, when really it is *us* making the wrong choices. That morning, hitting the snooze button five times instead of getting up, you slept in and ran late. The choice to sleep in versus getting on the road at the right time lost you the deal.

SO AGAIN, OWN YOUR CHOICES!

If you don't, they will add weight to your life, decrease your effectiveness and hold you back from what you want.

The toughest choices to make are emotional choices: family, friends, finance, and future. Why do people find it difficult to make choices around these four areas? The reasons for these difficulties are varied, but mostly involve fear, stress, personal history, and discomfort with the unknown. Many people don't want to deal with certain things, so they don't. The need to make choices and take action will sit in your subconscious until you are forced to make decisions quickly and with unease. When you're Results Map is clear, even these tougher, emotion-driven decisions come easier. This doesn't mean that you do not consider people's feelings or potential outcomes. What it does is help you approach these tougher areas with the ability to make wiser, more confident decisions and to take action from them.

So, how do you take normally tough choices and make them easier? Working with family, friends, finance and future can be as difficult as you choose to make it. Three words can change all this: perspective, strategy and results!

Consider these three steps when making a difficult choice in any situation:

1. Perspective: Assess the situation in black and white facts. Sometimes charting on a piece of paper helps. Take your feelings and emotions out of it. What is the current situation and what needs to be done?

2. Strategy: Now that you understand the full scope of the situation, look at how it can be handled. Maybe look at different approaches with possible different outcomes. Again, sticking to the facts.

3. Action: Now that you know what needs to be done and how you will handle it, how will you take action? Do you need support from other people or do you need to research additional information? Even in an emotional meeting, take a deep breath and keep calm. Stick to the facts and you will not only get through it, but you will be confident in your choices and in control of the meeting.

REMOVING THE EMOTION FROM ANY SITUATION AND STAYING MINDFUL OF THE FACTS IN FRONT OF YOU WILL ENABLE EFFECTIVE CHOICES TO BE MADE.

Growing up, my dad always told me, "Kimberly, it's a part of life." It is YOUR choice to change. Change can be scary and emotional. Understanding the steps you need to take to work on building your Results Map will give you strength to put your first foot forward, one step at a time. Have you heard the phrase, "Rome wasn't built in a day"? Well, neither was your business and life. Take it one step at a time. This is not a sprint or a marathon, but a journey.

SOMETIMES WE NEED TO MAKE TOUGH CHOICES AND DO THE HARD WORKTO CHANGE. WHEN YOUR TRANSFORMATION HAPPENS, EVEN THE SMALLEST OF TWEAKS TO YOUR BUSINESS WILL ALLOW YOU TO SOAR HIGHER THAN YOU'VE IMAGINED.

One choice can change the entire outcome of your business and life. But it all starts with you and identifying possibilities. Keep reading, you will find them.

MAIN MESSAGE

➢ Making the Choice to change is critical in either moving forward toward your planned accomplishments or holding yourself back.

➢ Keep emotion out of making choices

➢ You can strategically make choices and take action to change through the system of perspective, strategy and results

NOTES

CHAPTER 3
YOUR CREW

*"It doesn't matter where you go in life,
it matters who you have beside you."*
— Author Unknown

THE RESULTS MAP FUNDAMENTAL: PERSPECTIVE

In my career, I believed my strongest successes came from thinking strategically. I would assess opportunities in companies, develop a strategy and execute with measurable results. I had a love for the drive of the corporate world with an entrepreneurial spirit. What I realized is that my strategies were only strategies on paper; it's how you inspire, influence and impact people that move you forward. This chapter talks about the value of people and how without them, your success will more than likely be lingering on the horizon and forever out of reach. People make the difference and without them your Results Map would stay on the drawing board.

In the history of mankind, I have never heard of any one individual, company or empire making history or building greatness through the actions of one individual person. From start to finish, do you think anyone has really ever made it on their own? No trick questions here. The answer is "No." It would be almost impossible to build most of anything on your own, and why would you attempt to do so? It would be more difficult and far less enjoyable. Making decisions, being the creative, the heavy, the everything is tough to do on your own. You have heard the phrase, "It takes a village." Well, it does! It takes many people to do anything really. Stop and think about it. In any important area of your life; from building a business, raising a family, training for a marathon, moving from home to home, or making major business or life decisions, it takes people supporting you and collaborating with others to drive you to your end goal. That's the message I'm sending!

PEOPLE ARE YOUR GREATEST ASSET.

Whether you're an entrepreneur or CEO, have one employee or one thousand employees, work with a peer group, a team of consultants, or anything in between, you're in the people business. You do not need to have a team of people or possess a fancy title to be in the people business. I may never have one employee in my company, but what I do have is a crew of consultants, coaches and service-based experts that keep my business growing. I also have peers, advocates, mentors, networking partners and clients. All of these people are of incredible value to me both personally and to my business. My crew has respect and trust in me as I do for them. I hold all of the same roles as I just listed for other people as well. Collaborative to the core, my business has succeeded because of the people I strategically assembled around me. Some people may call this their inner circle, their executive team or A List. Regardless of the name, it's the same idea. I choose to call this critical, much-needed team "my crew." Any journey, project or grand goal is so much more effective and enjoyable when you embrace the people in front of you, beside you and behind you.

THE RIGHT PEOPLE MAKE IT HAPPEN.

What does this mean to you: "The right people make it happen"? Depending on your perspective, it can have very different meanings. It could mean you have a dialed-in team of people working through your strategies and knocking results out of the ballpark. It could be a support group that is supporting your state of mind to pursue your dreams or fight for what you believe in. The statement could mean you have a group of consultants that are so aligned with your vision that your business continues to grow. The right people making it happen could also mean that you have a community of peers and professionals you have surrounded yourself with that are your advocates and make a difference in your life.

At different times within my career, I have had all of these things. You have heard the phrase "You turn into the people you associate with." In my opinion, these statements are true. The company you keep and the team or crew you have assembled or adopted can define who you are and what you will accomplish. Ask yourself: are you aligned with the right people?

I'm going to share with you an example of how the right people can make it happen. In the midst of launching my company as a business strategist and speaker, I was given the sound advice that if I wanted to pursue public speaking, the best way in doing so is to write a book. I had ideas of writing a book in the past and agreed it would be a smart idea. Once again, I'm so glad I am surrounded by such brilliant minds sharing their wisdom. The book was an important element added to my Results Map.

I started writing The Results Map; I'm not one to question the experts! As I started framing the book, I continued to conduct workshops, work with people individually and help companies with their challenges and struggles. I also decided to start identifying myself as a speaker, accepting engagements all over town with just about anyone who wanted to hear what I had to say. I started spreading the word that I was writing a book to everyone in front of me. I knew I was a guppy in a vast deep ocean of knowledge. I needed to be known as a speaker and now an aspiring author with no idea of how to do it. Fear of the unknown was there, but my will, drive and need to conquer these challenges overcame it. In fact, the support I received squashed any fear or freeze that came my way. I knew I needed someone who had industry knowledge and was willing to give me guidance. One day I got a game changing email: the missing piece to my puzzle.

Karen Loucks Rinedollar, founder of the Denver Speakers Bureau emailed me expressing interest in meeting with me. Karen had received one of my brochures for a workshop I was hosting that spring from a well-respected peer and dear friend, Cathy Reily. In fact, Cathy had gone out of her way to give Karen my brochure and to advocate for me. There was no benefit to Cathy for doing this other than the joy of spreading the word for a friend.

My advocate understood my vision, my planned accomplishments, my passion, my work and what I stood for. Because of our relationship and her clear understanding of my mission, Cathy handed Karen the flyer, making sure Karen understood that she had to connect with me. Karen invited me into the Denver Speakers Bureau after our first meeting.

She became an immediate mentor and partner, enhancing my knowledge of the business almost immediately.

MY CAREER WAS ENHANCED OVERNIGHT BECAUSE A PEER BELIEVED IN ME.

So, who believes in you? Who would go the extra mile for you? Who is advocating for you? I advocate for so many people every day that not only turn out great work, but have the heart for success, for business, and for people. I get other people more deals and connections than I do for myself. But it all comes around. You have heard people say, "You scratch my back, I'll scratch yours"? In any business or personal relationship, it's about having each other's back and helping each other out. If you do a good deed, you should not expect something in return. The message I am sending is that if you take care of people openly and with passion to see them succeed, they will more than likely do the same for you.

Within your company or your life, think of the people that would walk through fire to see your goals and dreams come to fruition. It should be clear by now that striving for any goal on your own is probably not the smartest idea. You need support beyond yourself to take on your mission and vision and drive your strategies to results. Your crew is a critical part of your Results Map.

But how to find the right people? To assemble your crew and advocates there are four simple words that will draw people to you. The four I's: Identify, Inspire, Influence and Impact.

First, lets look at **Inspire**. The definition of inspire is to stimulate, motivate and encourage. This is sufficient, but I would add that to inspire is also to give someone a voice, and to empower them to be their best. Inspire others, and they will inspire you too. I am inspired daily by those around me that share different perspectives, fresh ideas and words of support. Have you ever met someone face to face, read their book or watched their movie and found that the experience shook you to the core in a positive way? The first thing most people want to do is share their experience with the world and how it affected or even changed their life or business. I am an avid fan of Brendon Burchard, author of *The Millionaire Messenger.* His book was so inspiring to me as I was building my company that I shared his book with at least twenty of my peers that I knew could use his advice. I was inspired to pay it forward. I wanted my friends, my advocates and my crew to have the same experience I had and to see success I knew they could get from reading his book. Imagine how your business could grow simply by inspiring others!

To **Influence** is to guide and shape. Does your crew understand your vision? Do they get your mission and planned accomplishments? Do you know theirs? Whether positive or negative, influence can affect your crew as a small ripple in a pond or as a massive tsunami. Be mindful of who is influencing you and the crew that you can impact. You want to influence people for the greater good and to enhance experiences, learning and positive outcomes.

To **impact** is to have a strong effect on someone or something. How are you growing personally and professionally from your association with your crew? What do they gain from you? When you think of someone that impacted your life professionally or personally, who immediately comes to mind? Remember the difference these people made in your life and think about how you can pay it forward to others in your life. The Impact you have is a big reason why your crew will want to move mountains for you.

Identify your Crew. Who would advocate for you without even thinking twice and to see your strategy become a reality? How can you inspire, influence and impact others to see your vision and their vision come to fruition?

In the next exercise, identify the people that make up your top ten crew members. Place a check mark under Inspire, Influence and Impact if you have made a difference to them in that area. Remember, your crew is a strong piece to building your Results Map.

YOUR CREW
Inspire Influence Impact

1. _____

2. _____

3. _____

4. _____

5. _____

6. _____

7. _____

8. _____

9. _____

10. _____

Download your free corresponding resources and worksheets for
The Results Map at www.KimberlyAlexanderInc.com

Main Message

➢ People are your greatest asset.

➢ Establish your crew with the 4 I's:

    ➢ Identify the people in your top 10 crew.

    ➢ Inspire others and they will inspire you.

    ➢ Influence your crew through experiences, learning and positive outcomes.

    ➢ Impact your crew with value within your relationship.

Notes

Chapter 4

Beyond the Horizon

"Having a vision is putting your stake in the ground."
— Carey Conley, Vision Building Specialist, Infin8nation

THE RESULTS MAP FUNDAMENTAL: STRATEGY

So, where do you want your Map to take you and why do you want to get there? There is not one person that would answer this question the same way. This chapter will explore the foundation of your Results Map and the purpose for building it. What you want, why you want it, when you will get it and who will get you there will lay the ground work for your Map. Without this understanding, all of the exercises and learning ahead will not matter. This chapter is where your Map begins.

Everyone has different ideals of what direction to head. The exciting thing is that business is ever changing. What is important now may not matter ten years from now.

OUR OUTLOOK CHANGES AS
WE GAIN EXPERIENCE.

What matters to you? Do you dream of what money can't buy? Is it status, having a family, recognition, a good title, time for yourself, love or friendships? Or maybe you want what money *can* buy: a home, financial freedom, jewelry, travel, cars, apparel, a business or entertainment? Maybe you want a little of both? Our desires are tempered by our life experience.

Before we jump into exercises and start laying down the foundation of your Results Map, I want to bring you into some perspective. Every exercise in this book requires perspective and will help guide you to building the right Map for you. Finding the right perspective may even seem tedious, but it is incredibly important for your long-term success.

This process reminds me of a movie called *The Karate Kid.* After being bullied by local thugs, a determined kid decides that he wants to learn karate to defend himself. He asks his neighbor, Mr. Miyagi, an expert in the craft, to teach him how. Mr. Miyagi agrees.

Weeks went by and the kid grew frustrated. Every day it was the same thing; countless hours of home improvement chores that never seemed to end. He paints Mr. Miyagi's fence with specific upward and downward strokes; side-to-side strokes were not permitted. Then, onto waxing Mr. Miyagi's car. He put the wax on in a specific circular motion with his right hand, and then removed it with his left hand, again with the same circular motion.

The tedium finally got to him. One day the kid exploded, charging Mr. Miyagi with wasting his time. He was fed up from being taken advantage of and for doing his grunt work, all the while not teaching him how to defend himself from the bullies that continued to harass him. Mr. Miyagi wasn't teaching him karate; he was using a kid who was down on his luck. But something remarkable happened. Mr. Miyagi held his ground and challenged him back. The kid responded with the exact moves he had been practicing while tending to his tasks, from painting the fence to waxing the car. Mr. Miyagi had taught him the foundations of karate. The Karate Kid learning the foundations of karate, is like you learning the foundation of your business.

UNDERSTANDING WHAT YOU WANT IN YOUR BUSINESS IS ONE OF THE MOST CRITICAL PIECES TO YOUR RESULTS MAP.

There are two exercises in this chapter designed to help you find what you want from your business and your life.

1. Identifying what you want to accomplish both professionally and personally.
2. The four W's: Finding the what, why, when and who of your planned accomplishments.

It's time to Brainstorm! In the first exercise, fill in the lines below with what you want to accomplish. There is no time frame, no limits, no minimums or maximums. Just shut down your brain and dream. I have mentored hundreds of people in the fundamentals you are about to learn. For many, this first exercise was the most challenging because we have forgotten how to dream. Take a deep breath and take your time. You don't need to complete this in one sitting. Keep coming back to it and add onto it.

First, brainstorm what you want to accomplish professionally on the first page, including volunteer time. Example: make a certain level of income, get promoted, start a business, or become a leader.

Next, brainstorm what you want to accomplish personally on the second page. Example: spend a certain number of hours per week with your family, develop a hobby, plant a garden, or finish painting the house.

Note: Planned accomplishments are essentially strategic goals set to action. Where you want to go and what you want. Words are powerful so use them wisely.

PROFESSIONAL ACCOMPLISHMENTS

_____

_____

_____

_____

_____

_____

_____

_____

_____

_____

_____

_____

_____

_____

_____

_____

_____

_____

_____

_____

_____

PERSONAL ACCOMPLISHMENTS

_____

_____

_____

_____

_____

_____

_____

_____

_____

_____

_____

_____

_____

_____

_____

_____

_____

_____

_____

_____

_____

_____

Next, circle or highlight three accomplishments you want to achieve on the professional list and on the personal list. Why only three? Depending on the planned accomplishment, normally three accomplishments are the maximum of what most people can focus on at one time. You want to set yourself up for success and will have plenty of time to conquer the whole list, even if it keeps growing!

There are three critical questions to ask yourself when choosing your planned accomplishments:

➤ Will it make a positive impact on your business and life?

➤ Will it make you proud?

➤ Without it, will you be fulfilled?

CHOOSE YOUR PLANNED ACCOMPLISHMENTS WITH YOUR END RESULTS IN MIND!

Now that you have decided on your three planned accomplishments, both professional and personal, the next step is looking at the four W's again: What, Why, When and Who. The four W's will continue to be your touchstone as your work your way through choice and change.

We will now identify what each "W" means and the reasoning and need behind each one.

WHAT

You have just identified what you want to accomplish in the previous exercise, both within your professional and personal life. These are your planned accomplishments and they will forever be evolving and changing. Before I launched my career as a business strategist, speaker and author, I had another business I was building. I had big plans for what I wanted to accomplish. As I realized my life was taking a different direction, I had to be very strategic and "real" with my time. My planned accomplishments changed very quickly. You can be fluid with your planned accomplishments should your overall strategy change.

WHY

I could write an entire book on "The why." This area is so important because it is your driver, your need and your inspiration that creates action. Your why will bring results. For example, I could say that my why for writing this book is to help people and companies reach their full potential. This is true. However, it is also to make a living by following my passion, be home with my family and live the life I want to live. See the difference? You don't just need one reason around your why. This requires deeper thinking to get to the heart of the matter in order to work toward the results you want in your business. Your why is usually deeper than just one reason, so keep digging.

WHEN

The "when" is the timeframe in which your planned accomplishments are to be met. You may be able to do a forecast, but may not be totally accurate until you work through a few more exercises. But, the answers will come. Be specific with a month and year. For example, don't write "in three months." Instead, write, "June, 2016."

THE MORE SPECIFIC YOU CAN BE, THE MORE IT WILL HELP YOU IN YOUR STRATEGY.

As you are embarking on your journey, your end date may change, whether sooner or later. Learn from this. Some planned accomplishments are too aggressive. Others give too long of a time frame that's "safe." Challenge and stretch yourself to grow faster than you have while maintaining a realistic end date in mind. Again with more clarity, determining time frames will get easier.

WHO

What person or group of people will help get you to your planned accomplishments? Do you know who they are yet? The reason why it is important to know this, is that you may need to seek out that person or group for knowledge, connections, a service, or level of expertise. We covered the importance of people and your crew in chapter three. In this exercise you will determine specific people that will help you achieve each planned accomplishment. These people may be a part of your crew or not. You may know that you need a certain expert to partner with you or need an identified service. If you do not know anyone in these areas, you will be aware that you need to seek out and find them.

For example, I wrote this book, but bringing it to light was a different ballgame. I spoke to many people that had published books, and realized I needed a mentor to walk me through the journey of publishing, PR and marketing. I sought out CPA's, lawyers, and business coaches for guidance on major business decisions. I researched the professionals; people like Brendan Burchard, Amy Porterfield and Tony Robbins to learn how they operated and reached a vast audience. I made connections through trusted and valued relationships, reaching out into different networking circles. I listened, listened and then listened some more, all to learn how to share my message.

Don't be the hero; there is no need to be. No one person on this planet is an expert in everything, so don't try to act as if you are. It is close to impossible to reach your goals alone. If you believe you can get to your planned accomplishments on your own, you simply have not gone deep enough. Back to the village....it takes one to arrive at your destination.

Your next exercise will take some time. Determine the four W's for your three planned accomplishments for both your professional and personal accomplishments. Take your time and don't race to fill in the blanks. This is not a task to be rushed, but an exercise that lays the foundation of your Results Map.

Professional: What	Why	When	Who

Personal: What	Why	When	Who

Download your free corresponding resources and worksheets for
The Results Map at www.KimberlyAlexanderInc.com

Congratulations, I know this was a challenging exercise. There is no right or wrong response. Sit for a minute and reflect on what you wrote down. You may feel that what you wrote down simply cannot be achieved. Stop that negative thinking. You *can* and *will* do this.

THE CHOICE TO CHANGE MAY COME EASY AT SOME TIMES AND MORE DIFFICULT AT OTHERS.

If you feel overwhelmed, go for a walk or call a friend to gain perspective. After you have been able to take a breath, come back to it. Remember, this process is a journey. Your answers will continue to come.

MAIN MESSAGE

➢ Identifying and understanding what you want to accomplish both professionally and personally is one of the most critical pieces to your Results Map.

➢ When identifying your planned accomplishments ask yourself these three questions: Will it make a positive impact on your business and life? Will it make you proud? Without it, will you be fulfilled?

➢ Identifying what you want and why will be your driver toward your goals. The when and who will get you there.

NOTES

CHAPTER 5

VISION AND STRATEGY

"If you can dream it, you can do it."
– Walt Disney

THE RESULTS MAP FUNDAMENTAL: PERSPECTIVE

You have talent and skill. You also have growth potential. This chapter will help identify how to maximize your skills and learn where your best growth potential is. You can have the best plan in place, but if you don't take action in the right way, the strategy is not worth much of anything. The same thinking can apply to planning. You may be a driver, a runner, a fighter to the core. Or, you may be calculating and strategic. If you have a weak plan or a great plan but don't know how to use it, you will never cross the finish line.

IT IS IMPORTANT TO UNDERSTAND HOW YOU THINK AND ACT IN ORDER TO WIN.

How do you plan and take action? This chapter isn't intended to provide a deep assessment of your personality. Instead, it will bring awareness to your actions and how you can maximize your potential.

To make my point, I'm going to share a story about Ann. Ann and I worked for a company that had several different sales divisions. Heading up those divisions were very competitive managers. All of them were hungry to be on top, to earn the bonus, to win the trip, to be recognized. You name it; every manager wanted it. In this particular company, most managers were extremely outgoing and self-assured, had no problem speaking up or even having stage time. It was a case of type A overkill.

Ann had none of these traits. Yes, she wanted to be successful, but didn't care for the spotlight. She was on the quiet side and took very different approaches to her business. You would find her most of the time at meetings buried in spreadsheets. She was analytical by nature.

One year, the company was struggling. Very few divisions were producing and stress levels were high. The company was pulling out all the stops imaginable. I designed a spreadsheet just to keep up with the overlapping incentives, bonuses and guidelines. "More, more, more" was the company's solution, and it was exhausting everyone.

Not Ann. Because of her more analytical approach to the business, she worked with her people to discover what they needed. She did the math and, instead of everyone pushing for everything, she taught different people how to push for different things, all adding up to the numbers *she* needed. She didn't win all the incentives, but she came out on top. She went for the big win and not the quick fixes. As a result, she quietly soared into the black and up to the top.

What's the lesson? Capitalize on your strengths and be aware of your opportunities for growth. Ann's strength was planning, and she used that strength by working strategically with each person in front of her. She stepped outside of her comfort zone getting in front of her team to inspire and drive them to win. She maximized her strengths while opening up to personal growth and her team won the gold.

What are your strengths and opportunities? Do not discount the importance of knowing who you are in order to win. It can move your business forward or hold you back. Taking an attitude of, "that's just who I am," will not work. With that mentality, you have lost before you have even begun. You may understand exactly who you are, but have you maximized on the traits and skills that you have? Do you need additional skills to succeed? There is opportunity in front of you, so check your guard (or even ego) at the door and open yourself up for growth.

There are two simple ways to identify your strengths and opportunities: Are you a Visionary Driver or Strategic Planner? Read on to identify your best strengths.

The Visionary Driver thinks at a high-level. They prefer to look at issues from a 30,000 foot view, with low detail and outside of the box thinking. They think big, delegate easily and have a "can-do" attitude. They visualize the end results, often without worrying about the details. For example, as a Visionary Driver you can see yourself running your first marathon, knowing it will take a high level of commitment, discipline and expense. You already have a full plate and need to find the time, but you know you will get there in ten months.

Below is a list of some traits of a Visionary Driver:

Visionary	Driver
Imaginative	Insistent
Idealistic	Assertive
Creative	Self-Assured
Inventive	Decided
Dreamer	Firm

The Strategic Planner thinks at a granular level, with high detail. They prefer to follow guidelines and need to be in their comfort zone to be at their most effective. Sometimes they hesitate to make a move without the facts. They prefer to work alone and plan each step first to see if the end result is possible. For example, when running a marathon, the Strategic Planner will chart the amount of time needed to get in shape, analyze work and life schedules, cost out the trip and consult with a fitness trainer before deciding if this is the right goal for this year or if next year would be the smarter choice.

Lets explore another example: If you visualize a pool, the Visionary Driver will get to the pool and run as fast as they can and jump right into the deep end, not knowing the temperature of the pool. Nor does this detail really matter to them. Swimming was the point of being at the pool, so why not just jump in? On the other hand, The Strategic Planner will dip their toe in the shallow end to measure the temperature and assess if easing into the pool is even a good idea at all.

Below are some traits of a Strategic Planner:

Strategic	Planner
Calculated	Organized
Tactical	Directive
Intentional	Cautious
Process-driven	Prepared
Policymaker	Developer

There are times that you need to just jump in and other times you need to first dip your toe in. Understanding how you plan and take action is the same principal. Bottom line, you need to be both to get most jobs done.

AWARENESS IS DETERMINING WHICH ACTION TO TAKE WHEN PLANNING AND EXECUTING AND IF NOT EXERCISED, CAN BE A DEAL BREAKER OR A DEAL MAKER.

So how do you plan and take action? Are you a Visionary Driver or a Strategic Planner? There are three lessons that look simple, but may be challenging to answer. Stop and put thought to answering these questions. The answers will give you added insight that you need to bring out the best in yourself and achieve the results you want.

List three of your best strengths being a Visionary Driver or Strategic Planner:

1. _____

2. _____

3. _____

List three traits you can work to develop that counterpoint your current strengths. Example: If you are a Strategic Planner by nature, what traits of a Visionary Driver can you work to develop? (Note the listed traits for each above.)How will you develop these traits in yourself?

Example: Trait: Planning
Development: Work with a business coach,
add time to plan in my calendar

1. Trait: _____

Development: _____

2. Trait: _____

Development: _____

3. Trait: _____

Development: _____

List three areas of value from having awareness of both types of traits.

Example: "Project tasks will be clear and direct with detail needed to complete them" or, "my goals will be met on deadline."

1. _____

   _____

2. _____

   _____

3. _____

   _____

Now that you are aware of your current strengths, have identified new traits for growth and understand the need for both types of traits, your next step is to put this information to work.

BEING AWARE OF BOTH THE EXISTING AND DEVELOPING TRAITS WILL SUPPORT YOUR GROWTH AND BRING YOU CLOSER TO YOUR GOALS.

Planning and taking action in the wrong way can hinder your success. Like the choice between jumping in the pool or dipping your toe, be mindful of when you need to work different traits to work through your Map. Some choices and actions will require more thought, research and planning, when others may need immediate action. Understanding your strengths and opportunities for growth will enable you to build your business stronger, quicker and with a higher level of success.

Your success starts with perspective and the understanding of who you are and where you want to go. Let's review what you have learned:

> Owning your choices and the benefits of clear decision-making.
> The power of change and why it is critical to your growth.
> People are your biggest asset and with your positive inspiration, influence, and impact will bring results.
> The four W's: What, Why, When and Who to clearly identify your planned accomplishments.
> Understanding of how you plan and take action to support your success and growth.

These tools are the foundation of your Results Map. You will continue to rely on and refer back to the learning from these five chapters continually, spot-checking your progress along the way.

Now that you know where you are ready to head, it's now time to discover how you will get there. Keep the pace, keep going, great possibilities lie ahead....

Main Message

➢ Understanding how you plan and take action to deliver the strongest results.

➢ Realize what your strengths and opportunities are for growth to get what you want.

➢ Establish steps you will take to better encompass both traits.

Notes

CHAPTER 6

CHART YOUR COURSE

"The essence of strategy is choosing what not to do."
– Michael E. Porter

THE RESULTS MAP FUNDAMENTAL: STRATEGY

You have laid the foundation for your success. The next phase of your Results Map will be determining how you will get there. It's time to chart your course. In this chapter, you will identify the right activities that will move you toward your planned accomplishments, while determining a time frame that makes sense for your business and your life. Moving forward, you will take the perspective of mirroring your strategy to time.

Would you drive across the country without navigation, GPS or even a paper map? Unless you have days to kill? Would you just get in your car and go? In my workshops and mentoring there is always that one token person that will say, "yes! Life is an adventure!"

But most people would simply shake their heads, with a look that suggested I was crazy for even asking the question. So, let's say that the one yes person was headed from Los Angeles to New York. They may just head east and eventually, they would get there. Is it really that simple? There are different highways and bi-ways to take, but which route will get you to New York in the safest, quickest, and most efficient way possible? Will you arrive in the amount of time you need to get there?

Could you plan your business this way? Probably not. Your business is no different than taking a road trip. You need planning and a strategy to get you to your end destination. Without a strategy, you can wind up even further off course, further away from your planned accomplishments, and, worst of all, you may not even realize or see it.

ONE WRONG DECISION OR MISSED TURN CAN TAKE YOU OFF COURSE.

Some of the activities you are engaged in now may be taking you away from your planned accomplishments. Assuming you have a current plan, you may be getting some projects done and landing some clients, but are you really growing as quickly as you want to?

Have you ever had a productive week scratching off the "to do" list tasks one by one? You put in twelve-hour days, conducted meetings, attended meetings, worked on projects and reports, all the while thinking you were getting ahead. But when you assessed your accomplishments at the end of the week, you had found that you really didn't complete anything? You thought you'd moved mountains when really you'd only conquered the first hill. What happened?

This is common across most professionals' calendars. Tasks do get accomplished. But are they the tasks that build businesses, grow teams and make bonuses?

JUST BECAUSE YOU ARE GETTING THINGS DONE DOESN'T MEAN THEY ARE THE MOST IMPORTANT THINGS THAT YOU NEED TO GET DONE.

I have seen this over and over again. The amount of time that you work toward a goal may not be as important as what you are doing in that time. You need to focus on the quality versus the quantity of work you do.

ITS TIME TO WORK SMARTER NOT HARDER.

You may have grown at warp speed but have hit a wall and can't determine why. Your current tactics will only take you so far. You need a strategic plan to chart your course based on what you want to accomplish, whether it be short term, long term or both. No detours, no scenic bi-ways; you have a business to build, a team to lead, and clients to manage. It's time to get on the expressway with your navigation guiding you to your destination.

Building your strategy may take you a day, a week or a month. It's important to take your time with the materials covered in this chapter. The exercises that follow will hold an important piece of your Results Map. Give it the time it needs to develop.

YOU ARE MAPPING OUT YOUR FUTURE SUCCESS.

Time to build your strategy. Let's start by talking about how you spend your time. There are two types of activities that we conduct on a daily basis: non-negotiable and negotiable. Identifying the differences between these kinds of activities is critical to your strategic plan.

Non-Negotiable Activities are high value, high urgency or high priority activities. They are critical activities that, if not completed, could hinder your planned accomplishments. They can be established weekly, monthly or seasonally. Examples of Non-negotiable activities are scheduled meetings, deadlines, grocery shopping, or paying bills.

Negotiable Activities are low value, low urgency or low priority. These activities, if not completed, would not hinder your planned accomplishments. These activities could be considered above and beyond required commitments or expectations. Examples of negotiable activities are: writing newsletters, perfecting your work environment (getting ready to get ready), working on a project three weeks early when another project is due sooner.

A very important point to be mindful of is that non-negotiable and negotiable activities can vary in status based on the time of week, month, quarter or year. When you are planning your strat-

egy in these time frames above, take into account that a non-negotiable task in one month may become negotiable the next month.

Listed below are examples of what can change status from
non-negotiable to negotiable:

Weekly: Meetings, presentations, networking

Monthly: Reports due, paying bills

Quarterly: Bonus reviews, sales planning

Yearly: Taxes, performance reviews

Now that we have defined what non-negotiable and negotiable activities are, let's review once more the categories that your
activities fall under.

Professional: Planning, networking, marketing

Household: Grocery shopping, mail, chores

Relationships: Gatherings, community activities, coffee time

Individual: Hobbies, classes, downtime

Rest: Reading, quiet time, sleep

Now lets start charting your activities. On the chart below, list
every activity that you complete within a months' time in each
category. In the "professional" category, be sure to list a minimum
of twenty-five activities. If you can't think of that many, try going
even deeper. For example, if you list "meetings" be sure to include
research time, planning, preparing, setting up and conducting the
meeting. That's five activities just for meetings! The same applies
to strategic planning, networking, reviews, etc. For everything you
list, think deeper into the smaller activities you must finish in order to make the big activity a reality. Do not worry about the
"time" column yet, just list the activities.

Professional	Time
Total	

Household	Time
Total	

Relationships	Time
Total	

Individual	Time
Total	

Rest	Time
Total	

The next step is determining the time needed to complete each activity within a week of time. Using the same form, review the items listed and estimate how much time is needed per average week. If there is an activity that you only do once a month, include the total time. If there is an activity that you do weekly, include the time not for the entire month but for the average week. Below are some examples:

➢ Professional: networking 4.0 hours

➢ Household: shopping 2.0 hours

➢ Relationships: gatherings 2.5 hours

➢ Individual: exercising 5.0 hours

➢ Rest: 49.0 hours

Next, total the time of all your activities in each category. Then add the time from each category to get a total amount of time. Below are examples:

➢ Professional: 120.0 hours

➢ Household: 35.0 hours

➢ Relationships: 25.0 hours

➢ Individual: 15.0 hours

➢ Rest: 49.0 hours

➢ Total Time: 244.0 hours

Notice the number of total hours in the example. Remember, there are 168 hours in a week. For your average week, we are now 76 hours over the actual amount of time that exists in one week. No wonder you are coming up short from your to-do list: you are simply out of time.

REMEMBER, YOUR TIME SHOULD MIRROR YOUR PLANNED ACCOMPLISHMENTS.

Some people may see similar results to the example above. Others may have time to add to their strategy. Either way, this knowledge will get you results. You are learning how to strategically filter what activities will move your business forward and what activities will hinder you from growth. But we are not done yet, onto the next phase of developing your strategy.

The next step is to identify your non-negotiables. Take a highlighter and highlight every activity that, if not completed, would hinder your business or your life. Then, go back and add the time up again. Understand, there may be some projects or activities that are seasonal. Most businesses have their busy and slow seasons. There also may be different weeks within the month that you are busier than others. For example, sales teams are busier at the end of the month, when training teams are normally busier at the beginning or middle of the month. Now start highlighting!

After you have highlighted your non-negotiables and calculated your new time, there are some questions to answer to spot check your progress:

- ➤ Does your time add up to 168 hours for the week?
- ➤ Do your highlighted activities align with your planned accomplishments and the 4 W's established in Chapter four?
- ➤ Do your highlighted activities align with the needs of your audience: your team, your clients, your partners?

Stop and reflect on these questions. Are you currently focused on the right activities to get you what you want from your professional and personal life? Does your use of time reflect this? If you need to stop and go back for review do so. This is your business and your life.

TAKE THE TIME TO MAKE IT RIGHT!

Now that you see the amount of time non-negotiable activities take, there are two options you have:

Option 1: You can **keep** the hours and time frames you have now to work toward your planned accomplishments based on the needs of your business and life.

Option 2: You can **adjust** the hours and time frames by moving your planned accomplishments based on the needs of your business and life.

These options get real with your time, determining the planned accomplishment and the time it will take to get it. You can now see how much time you have outside your non-negotiable tasks and the time you can afford to recommit to your planned accomplishments. You have identified what you want, why you want it, and who will get you there. What will come next is setting the boundaries of time that you are willing to work within.

Lets recap the process of developing your strategy:

1. List every activity you complete in a months' time

2. Assign estimated time to each activity with the average week in mind.

3. Identify your non-negotiable activities by highlighting or circling those activities.

4. Add up the amount of time only from your non-negotiable activities and get the total. Does the amount of time fall within 168 hours?
5. Spot check by answering the three progress questions listed above.
6. Determine your strategy choosing option one or option two: keep or adjust.

Take a breath. You have done incredible work! Feel proud in what you have accomplished and how far you have come. Your Results Map is taking form, so keep moving forward to make your planned accomplishments a reality.

Main Message

➤ What are the non-negotiable activities needed to work toward your planned accomplishments?

➤ Will you adjust: your planned accomplishments, or the time invested in them?

Notes

CHAPTER 7
BOUNDARIES

---

*"Don't worry about failures, worry about the chances
you miss when you don't even try."*
– Jack Canfield

THE RESULTS MAP FUNDAMENTAL: STRATEGY

Boundaries. They sound limiting, like they could keep you inside a box. However, with the right perspective and strategy, boundaries are really quite the opposite.

BOUNDARIES ARE SIMPLY
PROTECTED TIME.

Time that no one can borrow, beg or steal from you. Protected time that will see you through to your planned accomplishments and beyond. Boundaries will work for you, but require extreme discipline. Making the right choices of what you protect and what you let go will make the difference of the results you get.

In this chapter there are two things that will happen: First, you will continue to get real with your time. Second, you will put protected time into your strategy that you created in chapter six. Chapters one through five were your "wax on, wax off" phase of learning. You were laying your foundation and now will pull from that foundation for the rest of this book. Hopefully you will use these tools for the rest of your life.

Think about what you have learned so far. These may be concepts that you have never thought about before. We just identified your strategy and focused on your non-negotiable activities. Stopping for a minute, taking a pause in your busy life and thinking about what you want, why you want it, when you want it, and who will get you there is an incredible eye-opener. We talked about change, and how making difficult choices will take you further than you had dreamed. We discussed understanding the importance of where you come into play and how you plan and take action. Last, we spoke about your crew: the people within your business and life that can collaborate with and support you in reaching your planned accomplishments. Continue to evaluate your strengths and passions based on what you learned of them in chapters one through six. Go back and review what you have learned again and again as you are working through the next chapters. This learning will see you through to the end, I promise you.

Have you ever worked a tough week, ran yourself ragged, maybe ate three meals in your car three days in a row? Up at five, in bed by eleven and still waking up three times throughout the night, remembering what you didn't do? Or maybe you are so deep in reaction mode that you are planning your day three hours before it starts and not able to follow through on all of the great stuff you accomplished the day before? If someone else asks you for five minutes you just might crack. You look up at the end of the week and not a single project has gotten accomplished. Now you lose it and melt down. You worked hard, had a full calendar, attended and conducted meetings, and still do not feel accomplished or that you have even made progress.

"Buried" was the word I used to use. I felt buried, exhausted, mentally drained and felt like the to-do pile would never shrink. Does this sound familiar to you? Maybe bits and pieces of it do and, for most people reading this book, probably most of it. You get the picture.

"BE WHERE YOU ARE, OTHERWISE YOU WILL MISS YOUR LIFE" -THE BUDDHA

Applying boundaries to your time is a powerful tool for addressing weeks like the one I described. Getting real with your time is critical; what you plan to accomplish and the amount of time you dedicate to it, will make it happen. Let's continue your Map.

Boundaries and protected time are so important. There are four main reasons for managing your boundaries well:

- ➤ Keeps you on track with what you plan to accomplish
- ➤ Enables you to be proactive versus reactive
- ➤ Enables you to adopt a sense of balance in areas of your life
- ➤ Helps support healthy living

The first reason, keeping you on track with what you want to accomplish, will continue to resonate with you as we work through future chapters. Achieving what you want to accomplish will be easier for you if you protect your time with well-designed boundaries.

AGAIN I REMIND YOU, YOUR TIME SHOULD MIRROR YOUR PLANNED ACCOMPLISHMENTS.

I absolutely love this message and it really is true. Read it again, highlight it in your book: your time should mirror your planned accomplishments. Hundreds of thousands of people feel they are failing weekly, monthly, yearly mainly in part because of how they manage their time. People may have the skills to achieve their planned accomplishments, but the amount of time they commit to working toward them simply doesn't match. If time and activities do not match, you simply will not achieve what you have set out to do. Isn't it a relief realizing this? Your business strategies can now be formed into a black and white reality.

The second advantage of setting the correct boundaries is that you can be proactive rather than reactive with your time. Do you own your time or are you running behind it? Envision a train, a bus, or taxi representing time and you are running after to catch it. Have you ever felt this way? That time is literally running away from you? It's time to stop being a passenger and put yourself in the driver's seat.

OWN IT. CONTROL IT. GET REAL WITH IT. YOU WILL SEE RESULTS.

One more example: My husband calls me the Voicemail Queen. I am proud of that title. The reason why I love it, is that it is proof that I own my time. When my phone rings and I am in the middle of completing a project (and working within set boundaries to get it done), I will screen the call. Think about this: when you pick your phone up, the person at the opposite end now owns your time. Now, they may only ask you for five minutes, but wind up taking twenty. Or they might have some task or activity that they really need you to take on, but the time is lost and breaks up your productivity. This can happen day in and day out.

All of this is avoidable. You call the shots with your time. Protect it with all of your might and see what rewards come as a result.

The third reason to set boundaries is for a sense of balance. Why would balance be so important in relation to achieving your planned accomplishments in business? Balance will bring more meaning to your accomplishments and this will heighten every area of your life. Why make money, get promoted, start a new business, soar to new heights, but have no one in any area of your life to share it with? Balance will bring the perspective that what you are striving for is for the right reasons.

BALANCE DOES EXIST, IT IS SIMPLY A CHOICE.

I have had many debates around this subject. Some experts claim that maintaining a work-life balance is not possible, almost as if the very thought is a myth in business. If you want to get ahead, believe that you can take action and make choices in what balance looks like for you. One person's sense of balance may vary from the next person. It's about each individual person's perspective of how they want to live their life and put protected time around it.

The fourth advantage is gained from maintaining good boundaries on your time and your health. This is a big one and not often spoken about in the business world. A healthy lifestyle is critical to any successful person.

YOUR HEALTH HAS EVERYTHING TO DO WITH YOUR SUCCESS.

Sleep, stress management, exercise, even joy are big factors in how you perform in your job. Sleep renews your mind and body keeping you sharp, exercise relieves stress both mentally and physically, joy brings happiness and appreciation for all that you have in front of you. You owe it to yourself and your team to be on your game. You will deliver more and enjoy it more along the way.

So looking at the four results that can come from protecting your time with boundaries will bring you lasting results. What it will require from you is discipline.

The exercise you are about to explore will be easy for some and more challenging for others. You may have a perfect strategy in place. Realize that if you do not work through the tools and hold to your plan, practicing discipline, you will not get the results you desire.

It's time to get real with your time. You will be identifying your protected time within each category that we discussed in chapter six. How much time will you invest into each area of your life? There are 168 hours in a week and 24 hours in each day; no more or less. Review the five categories within your life once again:

1. **Professional**: Projects, research networking, planning, meetings, driving
2. **Household**: Laundry, the lawn, grocery shopping, post office, dry cleaning
3. **Relationships**: Family, Children, Friends, Partner
4. **Individual**: Exercise, hobbies,
5. **Rest**: Plan a minimum of seven hours of sleep per night

Next, identify the hours you will invest into each category in a week. Fill in the time in each box. The total number of hours must add up to 168 hours. Example: 60 hours for professional, 8 hours for household.

➢ First, identify the protected time and boundaries. If given a choice, how you would *choose* to live your life. These are your *future* boundaries that you will work to achieve.

➢ Next, identify your *current* protected time and boundaries that you are currently working within.

BOUNDARIES AND PROTECTED TIME

Future Boundaries

Profes-sional	House-hold	Relation-ships	Individual	Rest	Total

Current Boundaries

Profes-sional	House-hold	Relation-ships	Individual	Rest	Total

Time	Mon	Tue	Wed	Thur	Fri	Sat	Sun
5:00							
6:00							
7:00							
8:00							
9:00							
10:00							
11:00							
12:00							
1:00							
2:00							
3:00							
4:00							
5:00							
6:00							
7:00							
8:00							
9:00							
10:00							

Be honest with yourself. Can you reach your planned accomplishments within these hours? Reference the non-negotiable exercise completed in chapter six. If you cannot answer this question yet, don't worry, the answers will come soon.

Have you ever said, "I wish I had one more hour or one more day in the week?" Why are you asking for that extra time? Is it to do something that you love and enjoy, or to get something else done that you don't have enough hours for? Remember, your time should mirror your planned accomplishments.

Next, establish blocks of protected time with each category. Using the Monday through Sunday calendar, block out the time needed to fill the hours of each category in one week.

➢ Establish days in the week per category

➢ Establish hours within each day per category

➢ Ask yourself if you can achieve your planned accomplishments with the above set boundaries?

Example: You work a full time job and have decided to go back to school to change industries, get your MBA or learn a new skill. Your time investment to earn your MBA is:

- 20 hours a week, Monday – Saturday
- In class during the week, 6:00 – 9:00
- Homework on Saturdays, 10:00 – 3:00

This is an example of what you need to automatically add to your calendar and block out. You know you will be in class and need to get homework done. If you double book yourself, you may miss class or not get your projects and homework done. So note: if it is on your calendar, it will get done if you stick to your plan and practice discipline.

Now take a look at the parts of your calendar you blocked out based on the five categories of professional, household, relationships, individual and rest. Reference your non-negotiables exercise from chapter six. Does the time needed to complete your non-negotiables fall in line with the boundaries you have set? What needs to adjust? Refer back to your options: can you keep things as they are, or do you need to increase the hours or move the planned accomplishments?

So, how do you feel? I want you to stop and take a deep breath. Does your calendar look like what you thought it would? Can you fit it all in or are you out of time? Is your calendar so full you cannot fit in another hour? Did you add in more time at the beginning or end of the day before five and after ten? Do you want to make a change and live life according to the first set of hours you established?

No deflating here, this is your life right in front of you. Reality is staring you directly in the face. What you do with this information is entirely up to you. The good news is that the boundaries you want are within your reach.

Main Message

➤ Your time should mirror your planned accomplishments.

➤ Identify the boundaries that you currently work within and want in the future.

➤ Reference the non-negotiable exercise from chapter six and the planned accomplishment exercise (the four w's) from chapter four. Do they mirror each other? What needs to adjust?

Notes

CHAPTER 8

SYSTEMS IN PLACE

"In order to succeed, your desire for success should be greater than your fear of failure."
– Bill Cosby

THE RESULTS MAP FUNDAMENTAL: STRATEGY

Systems are methods used to effectively manage your Road Map. In this chapter you will learn how to establish processes from different timeframes to effectively manage your Results Map using daily, weekly and monthly calendars.

Having systems in place can be a deal maker or a deal breaker. You know where you want to head, what boundaries you are willing to work within, the people you should work with, and the right non-negotiable tasks to get you to your planned accomplishments. Without systems in place, everything you have worked so hard to figure out could simply vanish before your eyes.

Now that you have all of the right information in front of you, it needs to be organized so you can start taking action. What will systems do for you?

PROCESS AND SYSTEMS WILL BRING YOU PRODUCTIVITY, EFFICIENCY AND RESULTS.

There are three levels in developing your systems for your Results Map:

> ➢ Month at a glance: High-level view with low-level detail. Your plan and vision for the month (The four W's, chapter four).

> ➢ Week at a glance: Mid-level view with protected time (Boundaries, chapter seven). What you will focus on for the week.

> ➢ Day at a glance: Low-level plan by the hour driven around non-negotiable activities (Strategy, chapter six).

I have seen clients skip out on one or two systems, and when that happens there is a breakdown in detail. You risk losing sight of your planned accomplishments, sticking to your boundaries and making non-negotiables the priority. If you don't look high level, you miss the message, the vision, the plan and the end result you want to build. If you miss the mid-level, your boundaries, you will find yourself in reaction mode, out of the driver's seat and running to catch up. If you miss low-level or your daily planning, you are walking away from your strategy and non-negotiables.

IT TAKES TIME TO MAKE TIME.

You can set up these systems through your computer or phone, or a planner from any office supply store if you prefer. Let's get your systems set up.

Month at a Glance

> Set up your monthly calendar for one calendar year at a time.

> Add events to your calendar that are currently planned.

> Add tentative events to your calendar as they arise.

> You will review your month at a glance calendar at the start of every month. Some people prefer the last day of the month or the first day of the month.

> At the start of every month review monthly objectives: *events, vacation, business trips.*

> High level detail.

> Review your planned accomplishments to ensure they are reflected on your calendar.

See example:

Mon	Tue	Wed	Thur	Fri	Sat	Sun
30 Office	31 Comp Train	1 Comp Train	2 Field	3 Office	4 Kids Soccer	5 Open
6 Office	7 Board Meeting	8 Office	9 Field	10 Field	11 Kids Soccer	12 OFF
13 Office	14 Mgmt Meeting	15 Perf Review	16 Perf Review	17 Office	18 OFF	19 OFF

Week at a Glance

> ➢ Set up your weekly calendar for one calendar year at a time.

> ➢ Add events to your calendar that are currently planned.

> ➢ Add tentative events to your calendar as they arise, keeping in mind your established boundaries.

> ➢ You will review your week at a glance calendar at the start of every week. Some people prefer Sunday night or Monday morning.

> ➢ At the start of every week review weekly objectives: *calls, meetings, deadlines.*

> ➢ Set your boundaries as we did in chapter seven.

> ➢ Review your planned accomplishments to ensure they are reflected on your calendar.

See example:

Time	Mon	Tue	Wed	Thur	Fri
9:00 - 9:30	Admin	Admin	Admin	Admin	Admin
9:30-10:30					
10:30-10:45	Planning	Field	Field	Field	Follow up
10:45-11:15					from week
11:15-11:45	Calls				
11:45-1:15	Lunch				Lunch
1:15-1:45	Calls				Projects
1:45-2:15		Lunch	Lunch	Lunch	

Day at a Glance

➢ Set up your daily calendar for one calendar year at a time.

➢ Add events to your calendar that are currently planned.

➢ Add tentative events to your calendar as they arise.

➢ You will review your day at a glance calendar at the start of every day.

➢ At the start of every day review daily objectives: *calls, emails, social media, field appointments.*

➢ Set your planned accomplishments to your strategy as we did in chapter six. Does your time mirror them?

➢ Color coding can be helpful in daily calendars as well.

See example:

Time	Mon	Tue	Wed	Thur	Fri
9:00 - 9:30	Admin	Admin	Admin	Admin	Admin
9:30-10:30	*email, reports*	*email, reports*	*email, reports*	*email, reports*	*email, reports*
10:30-10:45	Planning	Field	Field	Field	Follow up
10:45-11:15	*month, week*	*ABC Acct*	*Blue Acct*	*Vendor 12*	from week
11:15-11:45	Calls	*DEF Acct*	*Red Acct*	*Vendor 10*	
11:45-1:15	Lunch	*XYZ Acct*	*Green Acct*	*Vendor 22*	Lunch
1:15-1:45	Calls	*Cold Call*	*Yellow Acct*	*Vendor 8*	Projects
1:45-2:15	*New Biz*	Lunch	Lunch	Lunch	*Sales Planning*

Download your free corresponding resources and worksheets for
The Results Map at www.KimberlyAlexanderInc.com

So what happens when the rest of the world doesn't follow your plan? You can have the perfect day, week and month strategically planned and in place. Sometimes business and life get in the way. Things like no shows, sickness, cancelled flights, and meetings running over can really mess up the best plans. When different activities are cancelled, often times we feel elated at the thought of the gift of time, like it fell out of the sky with a big red bow. You've set your daily, weekly and monthly calendars to reflect your planned accomplishments. You've taken those non-negotiables and put them to real time. You've set boundaries and strategies around those non-negotiables. Now what?

STAY IN THE PROTECTED TIME YOU HAVE SCHEDULED ON YOUR CALENDAR.

I cannot stress this enough. Stick to your plan. If a potential client doesn't make a meeting, and your protected time includes new business, you can follow up with other potential clients via phone or email. If your board member's plane was delayed, do some research on the industry, take a deep dive in analyzing trends, etcetera. Stay focused on work that falls under the protected categories you established in earlier exercises. Stay disciplined and the rewards of owning your calendar and time will follow. Of course, adjustments sometimes need to be made, but you can make these on a monthly, weekly and daily basis. Always spot-check your calendar to ensure that it mirrors your planned accomplishments.

Now that we are all systems go, its time to take action.

MAIN MESSAGE

- ➢ Establish your month at a glance calendar with your four W's and planned accomplishments in mind (chapter four).
- ➢ Establish your week at a glance calendar with your boundaries and protected time in mind (chapter seven).
- ➢ Establish your day at a glance calendar with your strategy and non-negotiable and negotiable activities in mind (chapter six).

NOTES

CHAPTER 9
LAUNCH

"You can have the best strategy,
but what matters most is the execution."
– Michelle Jones, President, Lulu Avenue Jewelry

THE RESULTS MAP FUNDAMENTAL: RESULTS

It's time to make the choice to change and take action! In this chapter you will crosscheck all that you have learned to ensure that every process is in sync. Making even the smallest changes can require great discipline. Keep the pace and keep going. Continue to work your Map to gain the results your desire, always remembering that your time should mirror your planned accomplishments. Lets launch your Map.

Although my belief is that we never fully arrive, you can sure keep growing and evolving. You have done just that and I commend you for it. You have worked through some challenging and maybe a little heart-wrenching work to get to this point. Like my dear friend Michelle said above, your Results Map wont mean anything if you don't put it to work.

LAUNCH YOUR RESULTS MAP WITH THE RIGHT PERSPECTIVE.

We discussed change in chapter two. Change is much easier when you are crystal clear in what you want and understand the steps you need to take to get there. Sometimes we need to make tough choices and do the hard work to change. When you choose to make positive changes, even the smallest of tweaks to your business will show different results. Make tweaks along the way. Your business will evolve as will your skill. You may need to go through this process quarterly. As my business continues to grow, this is exactly what I do. When I start feeling overwhelmed, I rebuild and tweak my Results Map. Like the flip of a switch, I am back on track again ready for the next challenge.

DISCIPLINE, DISCIPLINE, DISCIPLINE!

Many of these changes may feel uncomfortable at first. You need to break in new, lasting, positive habits that will bring you the results you are looking for. Discipline isn't easy. Jim Rohn says it so well: *"Discipline is the bridge between goals and accomplishment."*

With it, you can do anything you set you mind to do.

Have you ever seen a person going for a run in the middle of a snowstorm, the executive that returns every communication within twenty-four hours or the friend that skips dessert? Whether the smallest or toughest choices, these people practice discipline. Practicing discipline will move you ahead when working through your Results Map. The results will come when you stick to it.

As you begin to put your Results Map in play, there are a few things I would like to review:

➤ You are working to end less productive habits and create new, effective habits; it takes time.

➤ Choices of change can be challenging, however will bring you great rewards.

➤ Learn from your past to thrive in your present and future.

The balance of this chapter will be a bullet-pointed refresher on the choices and changes that you have worked through over the course of this book. We will review action steps needed in self-discovery, developing strategy, establishing boundaries, and building your systems. Every category will take an element of action required to see success. If action is not taken in any one area, it can break down your Map, your process and your results. Remember to take it one day at a time. If you fall, get right back up and brush yourself off. How do you eat an elephant? One bite at a time. The same can be said of your Map: take it one step at a time.

Self-Discovery Action Steps

➤ Assemble your Crew. Do you inspire, influence and impact other people? Do they do the same for you? (chapter three)

➤ Focus on the top three planned accomplishments in the professional category (chapter four)

➤ Focus on the top three planned accomplishments in the personal category (chapter four)

➤ From your three accomplishments, determine the four

W's: What, When, Why and Who. Are all of the boxes on your grid filled out? Do you need to do some research or network to find people to help get you to your planned accomplishment? (chapter four)

➢ Are the four W's reflected in your calendar system? (chapters four and eight)

Spot check: Do the five points above have a positive impact on your business and life? Do they make you proud? Without them, would you be fulfilled?

Strategy Action Steps

➢ Identify your non-Negotiable and Negotiable activities. (chapter six)

➢ Establish each non-Negotiable activity with protected time. (chapter six and seven)

➢ Compare your non-negotiables to your planned accomplishments. Are they in sync? (chapters four and six)

➢ Based on a 168 hour week, does your strategy match your boundaries? (chapters six and seven)

➢ What adjustments need to be made?

➢ Does your calendar mirror your planed accomplishments?

Spot check: non-negotiables and negotiable activities can change status week to week, month to month, or quarter to quarter.

Boundaries Action Steps

➢ Establish hours dedicated to professional, household, relationships, individual and rest categories for both future and current boundaries. (chapter seven)

➢ Cross check: Do these hours match your non-negotiable activities? (chapter six & seven)

➢ Plan days ahead in the week per category. (chapter seven)

➢ Plan hours ahead within each day per category. (chapter seven)

➢ Own your protected time. (chapter seven)

Spot check: Will you achieve your planned accomplishments with the above set boundaries and strategies?

Systems Action Steps

➢ Establish your month-at-a-glance, week-at-a-glance and day-at-a-glance calendars. (chapter eight)

➢ Review your calendar at the start of every month, every week and every day. (chapter eight)

➢ Is your calendar achievable based on the strategies you have created? (chapters six and eight)

➢ Is your calendar achievable based on the boundaries and protected times you have set? (chapters seven and eight)

➢ What adjustments need to be made?

Spot Check: perspective, strategy and results

Main Message

- ➢ Your time should mirror your planned accomplishments.
- ➢ Change can be challenging, but will bring great rewards.
- ➢ Discipline, discipline, discipline!
- ➢ Are your strategies, boundaries and systems in sync with your planned accomplishments?
- ➢ Spot check your progress with each step.
- ➢ Blank road map sheets to follow on the next page.

Notes

Download your free corresponding resources and worksheets for
The Results Map at www.KimberlyAlexanderInc.com

Professional:What	Why	When	Who

Personal:What	Why	When	Who

Future Boundaries

Profes-sional	House-hold	Relation-ships	Individual	Rest	Total

Current Boundaries

Profes-sional	House-hold	Relation-ships	Individual	Rest	Total

Time	Mon	Tue	Wed	Thur	Fri	Sat	Sun
5:00							
6:00							
7:00							
8:00							
9:00							
10:00							
11:00							
12:00							
1:00							
2:00							
3:00							
4:00							
5:00							
6:00							
7:00							
8:00							
9:00							
10:00							

Professional	Time
Total	

Household	Time
Total	

Relationships	Time
Total	

Individual	Time
Total	

Rest	Time
Total	

CHAPTER 10
THE JOURNEY CONTINUES

"Go confidently in the direction of your dreams!
Live the life you've imagined."
– Thoreau

THE RESULTS MAP FUNDAMENTAL: RESULTS

Now that you have launched your Results Map it is essential to monitor your progress. We discussed in chapters two and nine that change takes time and discipline. It is important to measure what is working well for you and what is not. Give each step time. I rework my Results Map quarterly as my business grows and needs of the business change. As a result, I am not stressed or buried. I am excited for what each strategically planned day will bring me. I have a lot to conquer in my business, but every activity that is a part of my business has a planned time and a day (or days) that I will work on them.

ACTIVITIES WILL GET ACCOMPLISHED BECAUSE IT IS IN THE PLAN, ON THE CALENDAR, AND HAS ACTION BEHIND IT.

The following questions are guidelines for you to measure potential challenges and improve results. You will want to review your self- discovery, strategies, boundaries, systems and action steps in the first thirty, sixty and ninety day time frames to ensure they are working for you. After the first ninety days and as your business grows, you will want to review your Map quarterly. You may add new clients, new team or staff members, or new processes. You will want to incorporate these changes into your Results Map to continue to experience growth and success.

To help you, I've included journal pages to monitor your progress during your first thirty, sixty and ninety days. I was never a person who wrote in a journal. As a child, I may have had a diary for a summer, but that's as far as I got. Two mentors that I highly respect had suggested that I journal once a week to write down my thoughts.

When referencing back, I couldn't believe the ideas I wrote down, the struggles and high points I experienced, and the learning and growing. Journaling makes a difference, so I am including it in your final exercise. I want you to journal for ninety days so you can track your progress. Write down everything. Write down your highs and lows; your successes and failures. Include learning experiences and quotes.

As I bid farewell for now, I want to thank you for taking this journey. Your business, your relationships, your health, your life will be better for it. Follow the fundamentals, tools and processes to make the changes you need to get what you want. Exercise discipline, choose to make smart changes and the results will come.

YOU HAVE ONE LIFE TO LIVE SO MAKE IT YOUR BEST. ENJOY THE JOURNEY.

JOURNALING DAYS 1-30

Have you assembled your crew to a minimum of ten?

Are you working your non-negotiable tasks first?

Are you owning your protected time?

Are your systems in place and allowing you to stay within your strategies and boundaries?

Has organizing your time increased your efficiency and results?

Are you focused on the right people?

Have you gained control of your business and your life?

Are your planned accomplishments achievable?

What adjustments need to be made?

JOURNALING DAYS 1-30

_____

_____

_____

_____

_____

_____

_____

_____

_____

_____

_____

_____

_____

_____

_____

_____

_____

_____

JOURNALING DAYS 1-30

_____

_____

_____

_____

_____

_____

_____

_____

_____

_____

_____

_____

_____

_____

_____

_____

_____

_____

_____

_____

JOURNALING DAYS 1-30

_____

_____

_____

_____

_____

_____

_____

_____

_____

_____

_____

_____

_____

_____

_____

_____

_____

_____

_____

_____

JOURNALING DAYS 1-30

_____

_____

_____

_____

_____

_____

_____

_____

_____

_____

_____

_____

_____

_____

_____

_____

_____

Journaling Days 1-30

Journaling Days 1-30

_____

_____

_____

_____

_____

_____

_____

_____

_____

_____

_____

_____

_____

_____

_____

_____

_____

_____

_____

_____

_____

_____

JOURNALING DAYS 31-60

Have you assembled your crew to a minimum of ten?

Are you working your non-negotiable tasks first?

Are you owning your protected time?

Are your systems in place and allowing you to stay within your strategies and boundaries?

Has organizing your time increased your efficiency and results?

Are you focused on the right people?

Have you gained control of your business and your life?

Are your planned accomplishments achievable?

What adjustments need to be made?

JOURNALING DAYS 31-60

JOURNALING DAYS 31-60

_____

_____

_____

_____

_____

_____

_____

_____

_____

_____

_____

_____

_____

_____

_____

_____

_____

_____

JOURNALING DAYS 31-60

_____

_____

_____

_____

_____

_____

_____

_____

_____

_____

_____

_____

_____

_____

_____

_____

_____

_____

_____

_____

JOURNALING DAYS 31-60

_____

_____

_____

_____

_____

_____

_____

_____

_____

_____

_____

_____

_____

_____

_____

_____

_____

_____

JOURNALING DAYS 31-60

_____

_____

_____

_____

_____

_____

_____

_____

_____

_____

_____

_____

_____

_____

_____

_____

_____

_____

_____

JOURNALING DAYS 31-60

_____

_____

_____

_____

_____

_____

_____

_____

_____

_____

_____

_____

_____

_____

_____

_____

_____

_____

_____

Journaling Days 61-90

Have you assembled your crew to a minimum of ten?

Are you working your non-negotiable tasks first?

Are you owning your protected time?

Are your systems in place and allowing you to stay within your strategies and boundaries?

Has organizing your time increased your efficiency and results?

Are you focused on the right people?

Have you gained control of your business and your life?

Are your planned accomplishments achievable?

What adjustments need to be made?

JOURNALING DAYS 61-90

_____

_____

_____

_____

_____

_____

_____

_____

_____

_____

_____

_____

_____

_____

_____

_____

_____

_____

_____

JOURNALING DAYS 61-90

_____

_____

_____

_____

_____

_____

_____

_____

_____

_____

_____

_____

_____

_____

_____

_____

_____

_____

JOURNALING DAYS 61-90

_____

_____

_____

_____

_____

_____

_____

_____

_____

_____

_____

_____

_____

_____

_____

_____

_____

_____

JOURNALING DAYS 61-90

_____

_____

_____

_____

_____

_____

_____

_____

_____

_____

_____

_____

_____

_____

_____

_____

_____

_____

_____

_____

JOURNALING DAYS 61-90

_____

_____

_____

_____

_____

_____

_____

_____

_____

_____

_____

_____

_____

_____

_____

_____

_____

_____

JOURNALING DAYS 61-90

_____

_____

_____

_____

_____

_____

_____

_____

_____

_____

_____

_____

_____

_____

_____

_____

_____

_____

_____

Acknowledgments

EMMA AND MEGAN, MY AMAZING DAUGHTERS AND biggest blessings on the planet. You are the smartest people I know and I learn and laugh with you every day.

Mom and Dad, there are no words for what you have instilled in me. You gave me a solid platform to conquer the world.

Elizabeth Almeyda, my baby sister, who believed in me and this project from the very beginning. Thank you Liz for your incredible insight, wisdom and for being the best proofreader and sister there is!

Michelle Jones, my forever mentor and dear friend, thank you for stretching and challenging me to a place I never knew I could grow, both in business and in friendship.

Kristie Keever, my Brand Manager and strategist, thank you for your incredible vision that has taken me further than I had ever imagined. I believe I have soared to new heights big in part because of you.

Polly Letofsky, my Project Manager and James Hallman, my Editor and Writing Coach, thank you for your passion and dedication to this project. I am so grateful to you both for all that you have done for me.

I have so many incredible people in my life that have touched me in different ways. I wish I could mention you all. Thank you to everyone in my life for your love and support.

29442078R00083

Made in the USA
Middletown, DE
19 February 2016